What you shouldn't do at school

This is a work of fiction. Names, characters, places, and incidents either are the product of the author's imagination or are used fictitiously. Any resemblance to actual persons, living or dead, events, or locales is entirely coincidental.

Copyright © 2014 by Joshua McManus

All rights reserved. No part of this book may be Reproduced or used in any manner without written Permission of the copyright owner except for the use of Quotations in a book review.

First print edition September 2014

Book design by Joshua McManus

Published by Imaginary Publishing
www.imaginarypublishing.com

Don't flick bogies
at the wall

Or go trumping
down the hall

Don't do a headstand on a chair.

Or ride on the back
of a grizzly bear.

Don't put your
head inside a bin.

Or play in
class a violin.

Don't dress up
as a scary troll.

Or wrap your head
in toilet roll.

Don't chase the teacher
with a slimy slug.

Or give the toilet
a massive hug.

Don't go sliding
on the floor.

Or hang upside down on a door.

Don't lie on the
table and go to bed.

Or wear your underpants on your head.

Don't dress up
as a silly clown.

Or drink fizzy pop upside down

Don't dance about
or mess around.

Or sing or scream
a horrid sound

But talking about sounds, what's that ringing, a sound we all know well.

It must be the end of the day and that's the school bell.

Well done if you remembered them all. Now remember everyone you must behave at school.

...The End

Read more by Joshua McManus

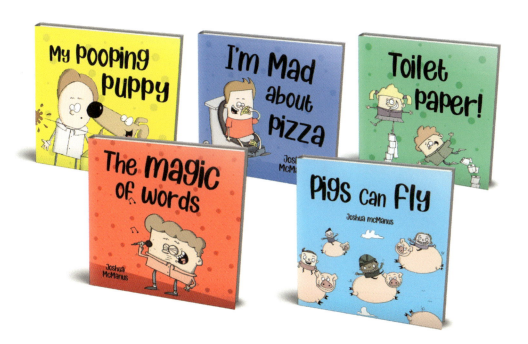

Printed in Great Britain
by Amazon